I0147178

Wilfrid Scawen Blunt

Satan Absolved

A Victorian mystery

Wilfrid Scawen Blunt

Satan Absolved
A Victorian mystery

ISBN/EAN: 9783337301095

Printed in Europe, USA, Canada, Australia, Japan

Cover: Foto ©Lupo / pixelio.de

More available books at **www.hansebooks.com**

SATAN ABSOLVED

A VICTORIAN MYSTERY

BY

WILFRID SCAWEN BLUNT

WITH A FRONTISPIECE AFTER
GEORGE FREDERICK WATTS R.A.

LONDON AND NEW YORK
JOHN LANE THE BODLEY HEAD
1899

DEDICATED BY PERMISSION
TO MR. HERBERT SPENCER

PREFACE

In publishing this poem, the Author feels that some apology is needed. It deals with matters of a kind not usually treated in modern verse, and which ask to be approached, if at all, with dignity and reverence. He trusts that he will not be found lacking on this essential point. Nevertheless, he cannot expect but that he may wound by his plain speaking the feelings of those among his readers who sincerely believe that Nineteenth Century Civilisation is synonymous with Christianity, and that the English Race, above all those in existence, has a special mission from Heaven to subdue and occupy the Earth. The self-complacency of the Author's countrymen on this head is too deeply seated to be attacked without offence. He has not, however, shrunk from so attacking, and from insisting on the truth that the hypocrisy and all-acquiring greed of modern England is an atrocious spectacle—one which, if there be any justice in Heaven, must bring a curse from God, as it has surely

v

already made the angels weep. The destruction of beauty in the name of science, the destruction of happiness in the name of progress, the destruction of reverence in the name of religion, these are the pharisaic crimes of all the white races; but there is something in the Anglo-Saxon impiety crueller still: that it also destroys, as no other race does, for its mere vain-glorious pleasure. The Anglo-Saxon alone has in our day exterminated, root and branch, whole tribes of mankind. He alone has depopulated continents, species after species, of their wonderful animal life, and is still yearly destroying; and this not merely to occupy the land, for it lies in large part empty, but for his insatiable lust of violent adventure, to make record bags and kill. That things are so is ample reason for the hardest words the Author can command.

To his fellow poets and poetic critics the Author too would say a word. He has chosen as the vehicle of his thought a metre to which in English they are unaccustomed, the six-foot Alexandrine couplet. For some reason which the Author has never understood, this, the classic metre in France, has stood in disrepute with us. Yet he ventures to think that, for rhetorical and dramatic purposes, it is infinitely preferable to our own heroic couplet, and preferable even, in any hands but the strongest, to our traditional blank verse. He believes, moreover, that if our skilled dramatists would make trial of it, it would, by its extreme flexibility and the natural break of its cesura, enable them to capture that shyest of all shy things—success in a rhymed modern play. At least, he trusts that they will give it their consideration, and not condemn him off-hand because, having a rhetorical subject to deal with, he has treated it rhetorically and in what he considers the best rhetoric form, though both rhetoric and Alexandrines are out of fashion.

Lastly, he has to discharge, in connection with his poem, a double debt of gratitude. The poem, unworthy as it is, is, by permission, dedicated to the first of living thinkers, Mr. Herbert Spencer. To his reasoned and life-long advocacy of the rights of the weak in Man's higher evolution is due all that in the poem is intellectually worthiest, to this and to the inspiration of much personal encouragement and sympathy received by the Author at a moment of public excitement when it was onerous yet necessary for the Author to speak unpopular truths.

To Mr. Spencer's great name the Author would add the name of that other senior of the ideal world, Mr. George Frederick Watts, the first of living painters, with whom, while the poem was in progress, it was his privilege to spend many emotional hours in high communings on Life and Death and the tragic Beauty of the world. He would thank him publicly here for the leave generously given him to add to the volume its chief ornament, the frontispiece, which is a reproduction of Mr. Watts' Angel of Pity weeping over the dead birds' wings.

To both these heroic workers in the cause of good the Author in gratitude inscribes himself their faithful servant, disciple, and friend.

FERNYCROFT, NEW FOREST.
July 27th, 1899.

SATAN ABSOLVED

A Victorian Mystery

✿

(In the antechamber of Heaven. Satan walks alone. Angels in groups conversing).

SATAN

To-day is the Lord's "day." Once more on His good pleasure
I, the Heresiarch, wait and pace these halls at leisure
Among the Orthodox, the unfallen Sons of God.
How sweet in truth Heaven is, its floors of sandal wood,
Its old-world furniture, its linen long in press,
Its incense, mummeries, flowers, its scent of holiness!
Each house has its own smell. The smell of Heaven to me
Intoxicates and haunts—and hurts. Who would not be
God's liveried servant here, the slave of His behest,
Rather than reign outside? I like good things the best,
Fair things, things innocent; and gladly, if He willed,
Would enter His Saints' kingdom—even as a little child (*laughs*).

I   B

I have come to make my peace, to crave a full "amaun,"
Peace, pardon, reconcilement, truce to our daggers-drawn,
Which have so long distraught the fair wise Universe,
An end to my rebellion and the mortal curse
Of always evil-doing. He will mayhap agree
I was less wholly wrong about Humanity
The day I dared to warn His wisdom of that flaw.
It was at least the truth, the whole truth I foresaw
When he must needs create that simian "in His own
Image and likeness." Faugh ! the unseemly carrion !
I claim a new revision and with proofs in hand,
No Job now in my path to foil me and withstand.
Oh, I will serve Him well !
       (*Certain Angels approach*).   But who are these that come
With their grieved faces pale and eyes of martyrdom?
Not our good Sons of God?   They stop, gesticulate,
Argue apart, some weep,—weep, here within Heaven's gate !
Sob almost in God's sight ! ay, real salt human tears,
Such as no Spirit wept these thrice three thousand years.
The last shed were my own, that night of reprobation
When I unsheathed my sword and headed the lost nation.
Since then not one of them has spoken above his breath
Or whispered in these courts one word of life or death
Displeasing to the Lord.   No Seraph of them all,
Save I this day each year, has dared to cross Heaven's hall
And give voice to ill news, an unwelcome truth to Him.
Not Michael's self hath dared, prince of the Seraphim.

2

Yet all now wail aloud.   What ails ye, brethren ?   Speak !
Are ye too in rebellion ?

ANGELS

Satan, no.   But weak
With our long earthly toil, the unthankful care of Man.

SATAN

Ye have in truth good cause.

ANGELS

And we would know God's plan,
His true thought for the world, the wherefore and the why
Of His long patience mocked, His name in jeopardy.
We have no heart to serve without instructions new.

SATAN

Ye have made a late discovery.

ANGELS

There is no rain, no dew,
No watering of God's grace that can make green Man's heart,
Or draw him nearer Heaven to play a godlier part.
Our service has grown vain.   We have no rest nor sleep ;
The Earth's cry is too loud.

SATAN

Ye have all cause to weep
Since you depend on Man.   I told it and foretold.

ANGELS

Truly thou didst.

SATAN

Dear fools! But have ye heart to hold
Such plaint before the Lord, to apprise Him of this thing
In its full naked fact and call your reckoning?

ANGELS

We dare not face his frown. He lives in ignorance.
His pride is in His Earth. If He but looks askance
We tremble and grow dumb.

SATAN

And ye will bear it then?

ANGELS

We dare not grieve His peace. He loves this race of men.

SATAN

The truth should hardly grieve.

ANGELS

He would count it us for pride.
He holds Mankind redeemed, since His Son stooped and died.
We dare not venture.

SATAN

See, I have less than you to lose.
Give me your brief.

4

ANGELS

Ay, speak.   Thee He will not refuse.
Mayhap thou shalt persuade Him.

SATAN

And withal find grace.
The Lord is a just God.   He will rejudge this case,
Ay, haply, even mine.   O glorious occasion!
To champion Heaven's whole right without shift or evasion
And plead the Angels' cause!   Take courage, my sad heart,
Thine hour hath come to thee, to play this worthiest part
And prove thy right, thine too, to Heaven's moralities,
Not worse than these that wait, only alas more wise!

ANGELS

Hush!   Silence!   The Lord God!   (*Entereth the Lord God, to
whom the Angels minister.   He taketh His seat upon the throne*).

THE LORD GOD

Thank ye, my servants all.
Thank ye, good Seraphim.   To all and several,
Sons of the House, God's blessing—who ne'er gave God pain.
Impeccable white Spirits, tell me once again
How goeth it with the World, my ordered Universe,
My Powers and Dominations?   Michael, thou, rehearse
The glory of the Heavens.   Tell me, star and star,
Do they still sing together in their spheres afar?
Have they their speech, their language?   Are their voices heard?

5

MICHAEL

All's well with the World.   Each morn, as bird to answering bird,
The Stars shout in Thy glory praise unchanged yet new.
They magnify Thy name.

THE LORD GOD

Truth's self were else untrue.
Time needs be optimist nor foul its own abode.
Else were Creation mocked--and haply I not God.
In sooth all's well with the World.   And thou my Raphael,
How fare the Spirit hosts?   Say, is *thy* world, too, well?

RAPHAEL

All's well with the World.   We stand, as aye, obedient.
We have no thought but Thee, no asking, no intent
More than to laud and worship, O most merciful,
Being of those that wait.

SATAN (*aside*)

The contemplative rule
Out-ministers the active.   These have right to boast,
Who stand aye in His presence, beyond the Angel host.

THE LORD GOD

And none of ye grow weary?

RAPHAEL

Nay in truth.

6

THE LORD GOD

Not one?

SATAN (*aside*)

God is a jealous God.   He doubteth Thee.

RAPHAEL

Nay, none.

We are not as the Angels.

THE LORD GOD

These have their devoirs,
The search, the novelty.   Ye drowse here in your choirs,
Sleep-walkers all,—while these, glad messengers, go forth
Upon new joyous errands, Earthwards, South and North,
To visit men and cities.   What is strange as Man?
What fair as his green Globe in all Creation's plan?
What ordered as his march of life, of mind, of will?
What subtle as his conscience set at grips with ill?
Their service needs no sleep who guide Man's destinies.
Speak, Gabriel, thou the last.   Is Man grown grand and wise?
Hath he his place on Earth, prince of Time's fashionings,
Noblest and fairest found, the roof and crown of things?
Is the World joyful all in his most perfect joy?
Hath the good triumphed, tell, o'er pain and Time's annoy,
Since Our Son died, who taught the way of perfect peace?
Thou knowest it how I love these dear Humanities.
Is all quite well with Man?

7

GABRIEL

All's well with the World, ay well.
All's well enough with Man.

SATAN (aside)

Alas, poor Gabriel.

THE LORD GOD

How meanest thou "enough"? Man holdeth then Earth's seat,
Master of living things. He mild is and discreet,
Supreme in My Son's peace. The Earth is comforted
With its long rest from toil, nor goeth aught in dread,
Seeing all wars have ceased, the mad wars of old time.
The lion and the lamb lie down in every clime.
There is no strife for gold, for place, for dignities,
All holding My Son's creed! The last fool hath grown wise.
He hath renounced his gods, the things of wood and stone!

GABRIEL

The Christian name prevaileth. Its dominion
Groweth in all the lands. From Candia to Cathay
The fear of Christ is spread, and wide through Africa.

THE LORD GOD

The fear and not the love?

GABRIEL

Who knoweth Man's heart? All bow,
And all proclaim His might. The manner and the how

8

It were less safe to argue, since some frailties be.
We take the outward act to prove conformity.
All's well enough with Man—most well with Christendom.

THE LORD GOD
Again thou sayest "enough." How fareth it in Rome?
Hath My vicegerent rest?

GABRIEL
He sitteth as of old
Enthroned in Peter's chair with glories manifold.
He sang a mass this morning and I heard his prayer.

THE LORD GOD
For Peace?

GABRIEL
And Power on Earth.

THE LORD GOD
And were the monarchs there,
The great ones in their place? Did all pray with one breath?

GABRIEL
Some priests and poor I saw,

SATAN (aside)
The poor he always hath.

GABRIEL
His guards, his chamberlains.

9   c

The Lord God

                 The mighty ones, the proud,
Do they not kneel together daily in one crowd?
Have they no common counsel?

Gabriel

                 Kings have their own needs,
Demanding separate service.

Satan (*aside*)

                 Ay, and their own creeds.
One cause alone combines them, and one service—mine.

The Lord God

Thou sayest?

Gabriel

Man still is Man.

The Lord God

                 We did redeem his line
And crown him with new worship.   In the ancient days
His was a stubborn neck.   But now he hath found grace,
Being born anew.   His gods he hath renounced, sayest thou?
He worshippeth the Christ?   What more?

Gabriel

                 Nay, 'tis enow.
He is justified by faith.   He hath no fear of Hell
Since he hath won Thy grace.   All's well with Man,—most well.

THE LORD GOD

"All's well"! The fair phrase wearieth. It hath a new false ring.
Truce, Gabriel, to thy word fence. Mark my questioning.
Or rather no—not thou, blest Angel of all good,
Herald of God's glad tidings to a world subdued,
Thou lover tried of Man. I will not question thee,
Lest I should tempt too sore and thou lie cravenly.
Is there no other here, no drudge, to do that task
And lay the secret bare, the face behind the mask?
One with a soul less white, who loveth less, nay hates;
One fit for a sad part, the Devil's advocate's;
One who some wrong hath done, or hath been o'erborne of ill,
And so hath his tongue loosed? O for Soul with will!
O for one hour of Satan!

SATAN

He is here, Lord God,
Ready to speak all truths to Thy face, even "Ichabod,
Thy glory is departed," were *that* truth.

THE LORD GOD

Thou? Here?

SATAN

A suppliant for Thy pardon, and in love, not fear,
One who Thou knowest doth love Thee, ay, and more than these.

THE LORD GOD

That word was Peter's once.

SATAN

          I speak no flatteries;
Nor shall I Thee deny for this man nor that maid,
Nor for the cock that crew.

THE LORD GOD

          Thou shalt not be gainsaid.
I grant thee audience. Speak.

SATAN

          Alone?

THE LORD GOD

              'Twere best alone.
Angels, ye are dismissed. (*The angels depart.*) Good Satan, now
    say on.

SATAN (*alone with* THE LORD GOD)

Omnipotent Lord God! Thou knowest all. I speak
Only as Thy poor echo, faltering with words weak,
A far-off broken sound, yet haply not unheard.
Thou knowest the Worlds Thou madest, and Thine own high word
Declaring they were good. Good were they in all sooth
The mighty Globes Thou mouldedst in the World's fair youth,
Launched silent through the void, evolving force and light.
Thou gatheredst in Thy hand's grasp shards of the Infinite
And churnedst them to Matter; Space concentrated,
Great, glorious, everlasting. The Stars leaped and fled,

As hounds, in their young strength. Yet might they not withdraw
From Thy hand's leash and bond. Thou chainedst them with law.
They did not sin, those Stars, change face, wax proud, rebel.
Nay, they were slaves to Thee, things incorruptible.
I might not tempt them from Thee.

THE LORD GOD

And the reason?

SATAN

Hear.

Thou gavest them no mind, no sensual atmosphere,
Who wert Thyself their soul. Though thou should drowse for aye,
They should not swerve, nor flout Thee, nor abjure Thy way,
Not by a hair's breadth, Lord.

THE LORD GOD

Thou witnessest for good.

SATAN

I testify for truth. In all that solitude
Of spheres involved with spheres, of prodigal force set free,
There hath been no voice untrue, no tongue to disagree,
No traitor thought to wound with less than perfect word.
Such was Thy first Creation. I am Thy witness, Lord.
'Twas worthy of Thyself.

THE LORD GOD

And of the second?

13

SATAN

Stop.
How shall I speak of it unless Thou give me hope;
I who its child once was, though daring to rebel;
I who Thine outcast am, the banished thief of Hell,
Thy too long reprobate?   Thou didst create to Thee
A world of happy Spirits for Thy company,
For Thy delight and solace, as being too weary grown
Of Thy sole loneliness—'twas ill to be alone.
And Thou didst make us pure, as Thou Thyself art pure.
Yet was there seed of ill—What Spirit may endure
The friction of the Spirit?   Where two are, Strife is.
Thou gavest us mind, thought, will; all snares to happiness.

THE LORD GOD

Unhappy blinded one.   How sinnedst thou?   Reveal.

SATAN

Lord, through my too great love, through my excess of zeal.
Listen.   Thy third Creation.   .   .   .

THE LORD GOD

Ha!   The Earth!   Speak plain.
Now will I half forgive thee.   What of the Earth, of men?
Was that not then the best, the noblest of the three?

SATAN

Ah, glorious Lord God!   Thou hadst Infinity
From which to choose Thy plan.   This plan, no less than those,

14

Was noble in conception, when its vision rose
Before Thee in Thy dreams. Thou deemedst to endow
Time with a great new wonder, wonderful as Thou,
Matter made sensitive, informed with Life, with Soul.
It grieved Thee the Stars knew not. Thou couldst not cajole
Their music into tears, their beauty to full praise.
Thou askedst one made conscious of Thy works and ways,
One dowered with sense and passion, which should feel and move
And weep with Thee and laugh, one that alas, should love.
Thus didst thou mould the Earth. We Spirits, wondering, eyed
Thy new-born fleshly things, Thy Matter deified.
We saw the sea take life, its myriad forms all fair.
We saw the creeping things, the dragons of the air,
The birds, the four-foot beasts, all beautiful, all strong,
All brimming o'er with joyaunce, new green woods among,
Twice glorious in their lives. And we, who were but spirit,
Envied their lusty lot, their duplicated merit,
Their feet, their eyes, their wings, their physical desires,
The anger of their voices, the fierce sexual fires
Which lit their sentient limbs and joined them heart to heart,
Their power to act, to feel, all that corporeal part
Which is the truth of love and giveth the breathing thing
The wonder of its beauty incarnate in Spring.
What was there, Lord, in Heaven comparable with this,
The mother beast with her young? Not even Thy happiness,
Lord of the Universe! What beautiful, what bold,
What passionate as she? She doth not chide nor scold

15

When at her dugs he mumbleth.   Nay, the milk she giveth
Is as a Sacrament, the power by which he liveth
A double life with hers.   And they two in a day
Know more of perfect joy than we, poor Spirits, may
In our eternity of sober loneliness.
This was the thing we saw, and praised Thee and did bless.

The Lord God

Where then did the fault lie?   Thou witnessest again.
Was it because of Death, Life's complement,—or Pain,
That thou didst loose thy pride to question of My will?

Satan

Nay, Lord, Thou knowest the truth.   These evils are not ill.
They do but prove Thy wisdom.   All that lives must perish,
Else were the life at charge, the bodily fires they cherish,
Accumulating ills.   The creatures thou didst make
Sink when their day is done.   They slough time like the snake
How many hundred sunsets?   Yet night comes for rest,
And they awake no more,—and sleep,—and it is best.
What, Lord, would I not give to shift my cares and lie
Enfolded in Time's arms, stone-dead, eternally?
No.   'Twas not Death, nor Pain; Pain the true salt of pleasure,
The condiment that stings and teaches each his measure,
The limit of his strength, joy's value in his hand.
It was not these we feared.   We bowed to Thy command,
Even to that stern decree which bade the lion spring

Upon the weakling steer, the falcon bend her wing
To reive the laggard fowl, the monster of the deep
Devour and be devoured.   He who hath sown shall reap.
And we beheld the Earth by that mute law controlled,
Grow ever young and new, Time's necklace of pure gold
Set on Creation's neck.   We gazed, and we applauded
The splendour of Thy might, Thy incarnated Godhead.
And yet—Lord God, forgive—Nay, hear me.   Thou wert not
Content with this fair world in its first glorious thought.
Thou needs must make thee Man.   Ah, there Thy wisdom strayed.
Thou wantedst one to know Thee, no mere servile jade,
But a brave upright form to walk the Earth and be
Thy lieutenant with all and teach integrity,
One to aspire, adorn, to stand the roof and crown
Of thy Creation's house in full dominion,
The fairest, noblest, best of Thy created things—
One thou shouldst call Thy rose of all Time's blossomings.
And thou evolvedst Man!—There were a thousand forms,
All glorious, all sublime, the riders of Thy storms,
The battlers of Thy seas, the four-foot Lords of Earth,
From which to choose Thy stem and get Thee a new birth.
There were forms painted, proud, bright birds with plumes of
    heaven
And songs more sweet than angels' heard on the hills at even,
Frail flashing butterflies, free fishes of such hue
As rainbows hardly have, sleek serpents which renew
Their glittering coats like gems, grave brindled-hided kine,

Large-hearted elephants, the horse how near divine,
The whale, the mastodon, the mighty Behemoth,
Leviathan's self awake and glorious in his wrath.
All these thou hadst for choice, competitors with Thee
For Thy new gift and prize, Thy co-divinity.
Yet didst Thou choose, Lord God, the one comedian shape
In Thy Creation's range, the lewd bare-buttocked ape,
And calledst him, in scorn of all that brave parade,
King of Thy living things, in Thine own likeness made!
Where, Lord, was then Thy wisdom? We, who watched Thee, saw
More than Thyself didst see. We recognised the flaw,
The certainty of fault, and I in zeal spake plain.

THE LORD GOD

Thou didst, rebellious Spirit, and thy zeal was vain.
Thou spakest in thy blindness. Was it hard for God,
Thinkest thou, to choose His graft, to wring from the worst clod
His noblest fruiting? Nay. Man's baseness was the test,
The text of His all-power, its proof made manifest.
There was nought hard for God.

SATAN

Except to win Man's heart.
Lord, hear me to the end. Thy Will found counterpart
Only in Man's un-Will. Thy Truth in his un-Truth,
Thy Beauty in his Baseness, Ruth in his un-Ruth,
Order in his dis-Order. See, Lord, what hath been

To Thy fair Earth through him, the fount and origin
Of all its temporal woes.   How was it ere he came
In his high arrogance, sad creature without shame?
Thou dost remember, Lord, the glorious World it was,
The beauty, the abundance, the unbroken face
Of undulent forest spread without or rent or seam
From mountain foot to mountain, one embroidered hem
Fringing the mighty plains through which Thy rivers strayed,
Thy lakes, Thy floods, Thy marshes, tameless, unbetrayed,
All virgin of the spoiler, all inviolate,
In beauty undeflowered, where fear was not nor hate.
Thou knowest, Lord of all, how that sanct solitude
Was crowded with brave life, a thousand forms of good
Enjoying Thy sweet air, some strong, some weak, yet none
Oppressor of the rest more than Thy writ might run.
Armed were they, yet restrained.   Not even the lion slew
His prey in wantonness, nor claimed beyond his due.
He thinned their ranks,—yet, lo, the Spring brought back their joy.
Short was his anger, Lord.   He raged not to destroy.
Oh, noble was the World, its balance held by Thee,
Timely its fruits for all, 'neath Thy sole sovereignty.
But he! he, the unclean!   The fault, Lord God, was Thine.
Behold him in Thy place, a presence saturnine,
In stealth among the rest, equipped as none of these
With Thy mind's attributes, low crouched beneath the trees,
Betraying all and each.   The wit Thou gavest him
He useth to undo, to bend them to his whim.

His bodily strength is little, slow of foot is he,
Of stature base, unclad in mail or panoply.
His heart hath a poor courage. He hath beauty none.
Bare to the buttocks he of all that might atone.
Without Thy favour, Lord, what power had he for ill?
Without thy prompting voice his violence had scant skill.
The snare, the sling, the lime, who taught him these but Thou?
The World was lost through Thee who fashioned him his bow.
And Thou hast clean forgot the fair great beasts of yore,
The mammoth, aurochs, elk, sea-lion, cave-bear, boar,
Which fell before his hand, each one of them than he
Nobler and mightier far, undone by treachery.
He spared them not, old, young, calf, cow. With pitfall hid
In their mid path they fell, by his guile harvested,
And with them the World's truth. Henceforth all walked in fear,
Knowing that one there was turned traitor, haply near.
This was the wild man's crime.

THE LORD GOD

        He erred in ignorance.
As yet he was not Man. Naught but his form was Man's.

SATAN

Well had he so remained. Lord God, thou thoughtest then
To perfect him by grace, among the sons of men
To choose a worthiest man. "If he should know," saidst Thou
" The evil from the good, the thing We do allow

20

"From that We do forbid! If We should give him shame,
"The consciousness of wrong, the red blush under blame!
"If he should walk in light beholding truth as We!"
Thou gavest him Conscience, Creed, Responsibility,
The power to worship Thee. Thou showedst him Thy way.
Thou didst reveal Thyself. Thou spakest, as one should say
Conversing mouth to mouth. Old Adam and his Eve
Thou didst array in aprons Thy own hands did weave.
Enoch was taken up. To Noah Thou didst send
Salvation in Thine ark. Lord Abraham was Thy friend.
These are the facts recorded, facts—say fables—yet
Impressed with the large truth of a new value set
Upon Man's race and kind by Thy too favouring will.
Man had become a "Soul," informed for good and ill
With Thy best attributes, Earth's moral arbiter,
Tyrant and priest and judge. Woe and alas for her!
Think of the deeds of Man! the sins! No wilding now,
But set in cities proud, yet marked upon his brow
With label of all crime.

THE LORD GOD

The men before the Flood?
We did destroy them all.

SATAN

Save Noah and his brood.
In what were these more worthy? Did they love Thee more,
The men of the new lineage? Was their sin less sore,

Their service of more zeal?   Nay.   Earth was hardly dry
Ere their corruption stank and their sin sulphurously
Rose as a smoke to heaven, Ur, Babel, Nineveh,
The Cities of the Plain.   Bethink Thee, Lord, to-day
What their debasement was, who did defile Thy face
And flout Thee in derision, dogs in shamelessness!

THE LORD GOD

Nay, but there loved me one.

SATAN

The son of Terah?

THE LORD GOD

He.

SATAN

I give Thee Thy one friend.   Nay, more, I give Thee three—
Moses, Melchisedec.

THE LORD GOD
And Job.

SATAN

Ay, Job.   He stands
In light of the new Gospel, Captain of Thy bands,
And prince of all that served Thee, fearing not to find
Thy justice even in wrong with no new life behind,
Thy justice even in death.   In all, four men of good
Of the whole race of Shem, Heaven's stars in multitude.

22

I speak of the old time and the one chosen Nation
To whom Thou gavest the law.

THE LORD GOD

Truce to that dispensation.
It was an old world hope, made void by Jacob's guile.
His was a bitter stem. We bore with it awhile,
Too long, till We grew weary. But enough. 'Tis done.
What sayest thou of the new, most wise Apollyon?

SATAN

Ah, Lord, wilt Thou believe me?   That was a mighty dream,
Sublime, of a world won by Thy Son's stratagem
Of being himself a Man—the rueful outcast thing!
And of all men a Jew! for poor Earth's ransoming.
Thrice glorious inspiration!   Who but He had dared
Come naked, as He came, of all His kingship bared,
Not one of us to serve Him, neither praised nor proud
But just as the least are, the last ones of the crowd.
He had not Man's fierce eye.   No beast fell back abashed
To meet Him in the woods, as though a flame had flashed.
He lay down with the foxes.   The quails went and came
Between His feet asleep.   They did not fear His blame.
He had not Man's hard heart.   He had not Man's false hand.
His gesture was as theirs.   Their wit could understand
He was their fellow flesh.   To Him so near to God
What difference lay 'twixt Man and the least herb He trod?

He came to save them *all*, to win *all* to His peace.
What cared He for Man, Jew, more than the least of these ?
And yet He loved His kind, the sick at heart, the poor,
The impotent of will, those who from wrong forbore,
Those without arms to strike, the lost of Israel.
Of these He made His kingdom—as it pleased Him well—
Kingdom without a king.   His thought was to bring back
Earth to its earlier way, ere Man had left the track,
And stay his rage to slay.   " Take ye no thought," said He,
" Of what the day may bring.   Be as the lilies be.
" They toil not, nor do spin, and yet are clothed withal.
" Choose ye the lowest place.   Be guileless of all gall.
" If one shall smite you, smile.   If one shall rob, give more.
" The first shall be the last, and each soul hold its store.
" Only the eyes that weep—only the poor in spirit—
" Only the pure in heart God's kingdom shall inherit."
On this fair base of love Thy Son built up His creed,
Thinking to save the world.   And Man, who owned no need
Of any saving, slew Him.

THE LORD GOD.

It was the Jews that slew
In huge ingratitude Him who Himself was Jew.
O perfidi Judæi !   Yet His creed prevailed.
Thou hast thyself borne witness.   If Shem's virtue failed,
Japhet hath found us sons who swear all by His name.
Nay, thou hast testified the Christian faith finds fame

In every western land. It hath inherited
All that was once called Rome. The Orient bows its head
Perturbed by the white vision of a purer day.
Ham's heritage accepts new salves for its decay,
And there are worlds reborn beyond the ocean's verge
Where men are not as men, mad foam on the salt surge,.
But live even as He taught them in love's noblest mood,
Under the law of Jesus.

SATAN

Where, O glorious God?

In what land of the heathen—and I know them all,
From China to Peru, from Hind to Senegal,
And onward through the isles of the great Southern main.
Where is this miracle? Nay, nay, the search were vain.

THE LORD GOD

It is the angels' hearsay.

SATAN

A romance, Lord. Hear

The word of one Thy wanderer, sphere and hemisphere,
For ever on Thy Earth, who shepherding Thy seas
No less than Thy green valleys hath nor rest nor peace,
But he must learn the way of all who in them dwell;
To whom there is no secret, naught untold, no hell
Where any sin may hide but he hath wormed it out
From silence to confession till his ears grew hot;

25

Who knoweth the race of Man as his own flesh; whose eye
Is cruel to evasion and the lips that lie,
And who would tell Thee all, all, all to the last act
Of tragic fooling proved which seals Man's counterpact.
—What was the true tale, think Thee, of Thy Son that died?
What of the souls that knew Him, Him the crucified,
After their Lord was gone?   They waited for Him long,
The sick He had made whole, the wronged consoled of wrong,
The women He had loved, the fisher folk whose ears
Had drunk in His word's wisdom those three wondrous years,
And deemed Him prophet, prince, His kingdom yet to come,
Nay from the grave new-risen and had been seen of some.
What did they teach ?   Awhile, they told His law of peace,
His rule of unresistance and sweet guilelessness,
His truce with mother Earth, His abstinence from toil,
His love of the least life that wanton hands despoil,
The glory of His tears, His watching, fasting, prayer,
The patience of His death, His last word of despair.
And as He lived they lived—awhile—expectant still
Of His return in power to balance the Earth's ill.
They would not deem Him dead.   But, when He came not, lo,
Their reason went astray.   Poor souls, they loved Him so,
They had such grief for Him, their one true God in Man
Revealed to their sad eyes in all a World grown wan,
That they must build a creed, a refuge from their fears
In His remembered words and so assuage their tears.
His kingdom?   It was what?   Not all a dream?   Forbid

26

That fault, that failure, Heaven, for such were death indeed.
His promises of peace, goodwill on earth to men,
Which needed a fulfilment, lest faith fail? How then
Since no fulfilment came, since He had left them lone
In face of the world's wolves, for bread had given a stone?
How reconcile His word with that which was their life,
Man's hatred and God's silence in a world of strife?
Was there no path, no way? Nay, none on this sad Earth
Save with their Lord to suffer and account it mirth.
And so awhile they grieved. Then rose a subtlety—
Lord God, Thou knowest not wholly how men crave to lie
In face of a hard truth too grievous to their pride—
To these poor fisher folk, thus of their Lord denied,
Came a new blinding vision. They had seen Thy Son
How often after death, no ghost, no carrion,
But a plain man alive, who moved among them slow,
And showed His feet and hands, the thorn prints on His brow,
The spear wound in His side. He had come to comfort them,
Confirm them in the faith, by His love's stratagem.
How if this thing were real : If this, that proved Him God,
Proved also themselves spirits, not mere flesh and blood
One with the beasts that perish, but immortal souls,
Even as we angels are who fill Heaven's muster rolls
And so shall live for aye? " Here," argued they, " it stands
" The kingdom of His Heaven, a house not made with hands,
" Wherein we too new-born, but in no earthly case,
" Shall enter after death." On this fair fragile base

Their sorrow built its nest. It gave a hope to men
And pandered to their pride. And lo the world's disdain
Was changed to acclamation. Kings and emperors kneeled
Before the Crucified, a living God revealed,
Who made them heirs with Him of His own glory. Mark
The ennobling phrase and title. No base Noah's ark
Man's fount of honour now, but God's eternal choice
Made of His human race, predestined to His joys
From the first dawn of time,—the very Universe
Resolved to a mere potsherd, shattered to rehearse
The splendour of Man's advent, the one act and end
To which Creation moved, and where even we must tend,
The spirit hosts of Heaven—Stark mad insolence !
Rank blasphemy proclaimed in Rome's halls and Byzance,
Through all the Imperial lands, as though, forsooth, Thou, Lord,
Couldst, even if Thou wouldst, raise this fantastic horde
Of bodies to Thy glory, shapes dispersed and gone
As lightly as Time's wracks swept to oblivion !
Yet all believed this creed. Space, straightway grown too strait,
Shrank from these Christened kings, who held Earth reprobate
Save for their own high calling. Heaven had become their throne,
A fief for their new pride, in which they reigned alone,
In virtue of their faith, above Time's humbler show,
And Earth became their footstool. All were masters now
Of the brute beasts despised who had no souls to save,
And lords too of the heathen doomed beyond the grave.
God's kingdom had begun. It compassed all the lands

And trafficked wealth and power. It issued its commands,
And in default it slew in Thy high holy name,
Thine the all merciful! Alas for the world's shame!
Alas for the world's reason, for Thy Son's sane creed
Of doing only good each day to its own need,
Of being as the least of these in wise humility!
Behold our Christian Saints, too proud to live or die
As all flesh dies and lives, their emperors and kings
Clothed in the robes of life as with an eagle's wings,
Their Popes dispensing power, their priests absolving sin.
Nay. They have made a hell their damned shall dwell within,
With me for their gaolmaster in a world to come
Of which they hold the keys! God's curse on Christendom!

THE LORD GOD

Hush, traitor, thou blasphemest. If things once were so,
'Twas in a darkened age, the night of long ago.
None now believe in Hell.

SATAN

                    Or Heaven. Forgive it, Lord,
I spoke it in my haste. See, I withdraw the word.
Thy Christendom is wise, reformed. None buy nor sell
Seats now at Thy right hand, (aside) grown quite unsaleable.
None now believe nor tremble—Yet is their sin as sore.
Lord, hear me to the end. Thou dravest me out of yore
An exile from Thy sight, with mission to undo
And tempt Man to his death. I had fallen from Heaven's blue

By reason of my pride. Thou wouldst have service done
Unreasoning, on the knees, as flowers bend to the Sun,
Which withers them at noon, nor ask of his white fires
Why they consume and slay. I had fallen by my desires
Which were too large for one not God, because I would
Have shewn Thee the truth bare, in no similitude
As a slave flattering speaks and half despises him
He fawns on, but in love, which stands erect of limb
Claiming an equal part, which reasons, questions, dares,
And calls all by its name, the wheat wheat, the tares tares,
The friend friend, the foe foe. Thou wast displeased at this,
And deemed I envied Man his portion in Thy bliss,
The Man that Thou hadst made and in Thy royal faith
Held worthy of all trust, Thy lord of life and death,
One to be proved and tried, as gold is tried by fire,
And fare the purer forth. Of me Thou didst require
The sad task of his tempting. I, forsooth, must sue
And prompt to evil deeds, make the false thought seem true,
The true thought false, that he, thus proved, thus tried, might turn
And hurl me a dog's word, as Jesus did, in scorn
" Get thee behind Me, Satan ! " To this penance chained
I bowed me in despair, as Thou, Lord, hadst ordained,
Cast out from Thee and cursed. It was a rueful task
For one who had known *Thee* to wear the felon's mask
And tempt this piteous child to his base sins of greed,
His lusts ignoble, crimes how prompt in act and deed,
To urge him to rebellion against God and good

Who needed none to urge. His savage simian blood
Flamed at a word, a sign. He lied, he thieved, he slew,
By instinct of his birth. No virtue but he knew
Its countervice and foil, without my wit to aid.
No fair thought but he chose the foul thought in its stead.
Ah sad primæval race! Thou saidst it was not Man
This thing armed with the stone which through thy forests ran,
Intent to snare and slay. Not Man the senseless knave
Who struck fire from his flint to burn Thy gorses brave,
Thy heaths for his lean kine, who, being the one unclean,
Defiled thy flower-sweet Earth with ordure heaps obscene
To plant his rice, his rye. Not Man, saidst Thou, because
He knew not of Thy way nor had he learned Thy laws,
And was stark savage still. Not Man? Behold to-day
Thy tamed Man as he lives, Thy Son of Japhet, nay
Thy new true-Christened King, the follower of Thy Christ,
Who sweareth by Thy name and his own mailéd fist
That Thou art Lord of all and he the Lord of Thee,
Heaven's instrument ordained to teach integrity.
Thinkest Thou the *man* is changed, the *ape* that in him is
Because his limbs are clothed which went in shamelessness?
Are his lusts bridled more because his parts are hid?
Nay, Lord, he doeth to-day as those forefathers did,
Only in greater guile. I will tell Thee his full worth,
This Man's, the latest born, Thy creature from his birth
Who lords it now, a king, this white Man's who hath pressed
All Earth to his sole bondage and supreme behest,

31

This Man of all Mankind. Behold him in Thy place,
Administering the World, vicegerent of Thy grace
And agent named of Thee, the symbol and the sign
Of Thy high will on Earth and purposing divine,
Clothed in his robes of power. Whence was he? What is he
That he asserteth thus his hand's supremacy?
His lineage what? Nay, Lord, he cometh of that mad stem
Harder in act than Ham's, more subtle than of Shem,
The red Japhetic stock of the bare plains which rolled
A base born horde on Rome erewhile in lust of gold,
Tide following tide, the Goth, Gaul, Vandal, Lombard, Hun,
Spewed forth from the white North to new dominion
In the fair southern lands, with famine at their heel
And rapine in their van, armed to the lips with steel.
These made their spoil of all, the pomp of the world's power,
Its wealth, its beauty stored, all Rome's imperial dower,
Her long renown, her skill, her art, her cultured fame,
And with the rest her faiths bearing the Christian name.
From this wild bitter root of violent lust and greed
New Christendom upsprang, a pagan blood-stained creed,
Pagan in spite of Christ, for the old gods cast down
Still ruled it in men's hearts and lured them to renown,
Ay in Thy name, Lord God, by glamour of the sword,
And for Thy dead Son's sake, as in the days abhorred.
Like bulls they strove, they slew, like wolves they seized the prey,
The hungriest strongest first, and who should say them nay.
After the Goth the Gaul, after the Gaul the Dane,

Kings in descent from Thor, peace sued to them in vain.
Thou knowest, Lord God, their story.   It is writ in blood,
The blood of beast and man, by their brute hands subdued,
Down to the latest born, the hungriest of the pack,
The master wolf of all men call the Sassenach,
The Anglo-Norman dog, who goeth by land and sea
As his forefathers went in chartered piracy,
Death, fire in his right hand.

THE LORD GOD
                Satan, once more beware.
Thy tongue hath a wide license, yet it runneth far.
This Anglo-Saxon man hath a fair name with some.
He standeth in brave repute, a priest of Christendom,
First in civility, so say the Angel host
Who speak of him with awe as one that merits most.

SATAN
The Angels fear him, Lord.

THE LORD GOD
            How fear?

SATAN
                They fear his tongue,
Unscrupulous to speak, the right he hath in wrong,
The wrong he hath in right.   They doubt he hath Thine ear,
Lord of the Universe.   They are excused of fear.

They see his long success, his victory over good,
They count the nations lost which were of kindlier blood
But could not stand before him, his great subtlety,
His skill in the arts, the crafts.   They mark the powers that be
In earth, air, water, fire, all banded in his plan
And used to the world's hurt as never yet by Man.
They look on Thee, Lord God, as one that careth not,
On him as Thy supplanter and the iron as hot
Which shall reforge the chain by which the Earth is bound.
They fear to awaken Thee from Thy long sleep profound.
He hath become their God, one impious and profane,
But strong and unreproved, ascendant on Thy wane.
They kneel to the new comer as all courtiers use
Who fear a change of king.   Their news is an ill news,
Nay, Lord, 'tis but a lie.   I know it well, their story.
'Tis but the man's own boast, his mouthings of vain glory
Repeated day by day with long reiterate stress,
Till the world half believes in sheer ear-weariness,
And they, who think to please, retail it as their own.
What say they of him, Lord?   That he hath one God alone,
Is not as the lewd nations, keepeth Thy Sabbath holy,
Nor Thy name vainly taketh in the ways of folly,
Hath a wise polity—his Church and State close blent,
A lordly bench of bishops, peers of Parliament,
A Convocation House which yearly witnesseth
A king by grace of God, Defender of the Faith,
Thy ten commandments set in all his Courts of Law.

They show his fanes restored by highway, hedge and shaw,
His missions to the Jews, his Church societies,
The zeal of his free sects, each than the rest more wise,
The wealth of his chief priests, his weekly public prayer,
Things proving him devout more than the nations are.
They cite his worldly worth, his virtue these beyond,
His high repute in trade, his word held as his bond,
The valour of his dealings, his long boast of truth,
The prudent continence of his unwedded youth,
Uxorious faith in marriage, husband of one wife,
Nor taking her next sister to his widowed life.
These tales they hear and bring, some true, some false, but all
Of the common Saxon brag for first original.
So too of his world-science, social schemes, reforms,
His school-boards, gaols new systemed, signalling of storms,
Posts, railways, Homes for orphans, Charities organised,
His Mansion House funds floated, alms economised,
His hospitals, museums, baths, parks, workhouses,
And that last glorious marvel, his free Daily Press.
A wonderful Saxon truly, each day interviewed
By his own wondering self and found exceeding good.
All this and more they cite.   That he hath virtues, well,
Let it be granted him.   Those pay who most would sell,
And more who most would buy.   Alms to his credit stand
In his account with time, and add strength to his hand,
Serving his best advantage in the enlarged domain
Of his Man's selfishness, which works for the World's bane

More surely than his vices. He hath outlived the day
Of the old single graspings, where each went his way
Alone to plunder all. He hath learned to curb his lusts
Somewhat, to smooth his brawls, to guide his passionate gusts
His cry of " mine, mine, mine " in inarticulate wrath.
He dareth not make raid on goods his next friend hath
With open violence, nor loose his hand to steal,
Save in community and for the common weal
'Twixt Saxon man and man. He is more congruous grown,
Holding a subtler plan to make the world his own
By organised self-seeking in the paths of power.
He is new drilled to wait. He knoweth his appointed hour
And his appointed prey. Of all he maketh tool,
Even of his own sad virtues, to cajole and rule,
Even of Thee, Lord God.—I will expound this thing,
The creed of these white thieves which boast of Thee, their king,
As partner in their crimes. The head knaves of the horde,
Those who inspire the rest and give the masterword,
The leaders of their thought, their lords political,
Sages, kings, poets, priests, in their hearts one and all—
For all their faith avowed and their lip service done
In face of Thy high fires each day beneath the sun—
Ay, and their prelates too, their men of godliest worth,
Believe no word of Thee as master of their Earth,
Controller of their acts, no word of Thy high right,
To bend men to obedience and at need to smite,
No word of Thy true law, the enforcement of Thy peace,

Thy all-deciding arm in the world's policies.
They ignore Thee on the Earth.   They grant Thee, as their
    "God,"
The kingdom of the heavens, seeing it a realm untrod,
Untreadable by man, a space, a *res nullius*
Or No-Man's Land, which they as loyal men and pious
Leave and assign to Thee to deal with as Thou wilt,
To hold as Thy strong throne or loose as water spilt,
For sun and wind to gather in the wastes of air.
Whether of a truth Thou *art* they know not, Lord, nor care;
Only they name Thee " God," and pay Thee their prayers vain,
As dormant over-lord and pensioned suzerain,
The mediatised blind monarch of a world, outgrown
Of its faith's swaddling clothes, which wills to walk alone.
The Earth not so.   'Tis theirs, the prize of the strong hand,
The strongest being their own by sea alike and land.
" Thy Will be done," they cry, " Father which art in Heaven,"
(Where Thou canst harm nor hurt not one day in the seven.)
And if they add "on Earth " they deem Thee impotent,
Seeing Thee drowse thus long and leave men to their bent.
They mean " Thy Will in Heaven," or in their ",World to come."
" Terram autem dedit filiis hominum."
So think their chiefs, their lords.   For the blind mass of men,
Which live and toil and die heart-hungry in their pen,
They have no god but gold, the lord of their distress,
And gold's slave, drink, that buys a night's forgetfulness.
Of Thee they have no heed to chide them or to cheer,

37

The fear of Thee with these is their law's officer.
Lord God, if Thou but saw the pagan hearts they hide,
The base greeds of their being, the lusts undenied,
The Mammons that they worship ! But Thou dost not see,
Or Thou hadst purged long since this worst profanity
From the World's better way and thereby saved Thy name
Profaned in their foul mouths from its long daily shame.
Thou dost not hear, nor see. The smoke of their foul dens
Broodeth on Thy fair Earth as a black pestilence,
Hiding the kind day's eye. No flower, no grass there groweth,
Only their engines' dung which the fierce furnace throweth.
Their presence poisoneth all and maketh all unclean.
Thy streams they have made sewers for their dyes aniline.
No fish therein may swim, no frog, no worm may crawl,
No snail for grime may build her house within their wall.
Thy beasts they have enslaved in blindness underground.
The voice of birds that sang to them is a lost sound.
Nay, they have tarred Time's features, pock-marked Nature's face,
Brought all to the same jakes with their own lack of grace.
In all Thy living World there is no sentient thing
Polluteth and defileth as this Saxon king,
This intellectual lord and sage of the new quest,
The only wanton he that fouleth his own nest.
And still his boast goeth forth. Nay, Lord, 'tis shame to Thee
This slave, being what he is, should ape divinity,
The poorest saddest drudge, the least joy-lifted heart
In all a World where tears are sold in open mart,

That he should stand, Thy choice, to preach Thy law, and set
His impress on the Earth in full apostolate,
Thy missioner and priest. He goeth among the nations,
Saith he, to spread Thy truth, to preach Thy law of patience,
To glorify Thy name! Not selfishly, forsooth,
But for their own more good, to open them the truth,
To teach them happiness, to civilise, to save,
To smite down the oppressor and make free the slave.
To bear the " White Man's Burden," which he yearns to take
On his white Saxon back for his white conscience sake.
Huge impudent imposture!—Lord, there were fair lands
Once on Thy Earth, brave hills, bright isles, sweet coral strands,
Noble savannahs, plains of limitless waving green,
Lakes girt with giant forests, continents unseen,
Unknown by these white thieves, where men lived in the way
Of Thy good natural law with Thy free beasts at play
And partners with Thy birds, men who nor toiled nor span,
Nor sowed, nor reaped, nor delved for the red curse of Man,
The gold that kills the soul, who knew nought of the fire
Which in his guns he storeth, naught of the desire
More deadly still concealed in his fire drink of death;
Who went unclothed, unshamed, for garment a flower wreath;
Whose women lived unsold and loved their natural kin,
Nor gave aught to the stranger in the wage of sin;
Who blessed Thee for their babes and through the woods, like Eve,
Wandered in happy laughter, glorying to conceive.
Yea, Lord, and there were others,—shut communities

39

Of souls still on Thy path and strange to the new lies,
Yet, not as these were, wild, but held in discipline
Of orderly commandment, servants true of Thine
And doers of Thy law, but ignorant, untaught
Save by an inward grace of self-restraining thought
And light intuitive. No shedders they of blood,
But with all creatures friends, with men in brotherhood,
Blameless of wine, of strife. .In innocent arts well skilled
But schoolless of all guile as an unchristened child.
To these with mouthings fine come the white gospellers,
Our Saxon mission-men black coated to the ears.
"Which be your gods?" ask they ; "Do ye adore the Christ?
"Know ye the Three in One, or walk ye in the mist?"
"Sirs, we have One, not Three. Our poor ancestral wit
"Encompasseth no more." "Then be ye damned for it.
"This is our Bible, read. In the long after-death
"Ye shall be burned with fire. It is God's self that saith."
"We do not live again." "In this life, ye shall live
"According to our gospel, nor profanely wive
"Save with one spouse alone." "Our law hath given us three.
"Three Gods to one sole wife were multiplicity."
"These pagans are blasphemers! Who is on our side?
"See, we have gold to give. We may not be denied."
And they baptise them Christians. Cometh the trader next,
His bible too in hand, its free-trade for his text.
He teacheth them to buy.—"We nothing need." "Yet take.
"The want will come anon and keep your wits awake.

"Here are the goods we sell, cloth, firelocks, powder, rum,
"Ye shall go clothed like lords, like kings of Christendom."
"We live best naked." "Fie."—"We have no use for arms.
"The fire drink is forbid." "The thing forbid hath charms.
"Nay. We will make you men, soldiers to brawl and fight
"As all good Christians use, and God defend the right.
"The drink will give you courage. Take it. 'Tis the sign
"Of manhood orthodox, its sacramental wine,
"Or how can you be worthy your new Christian creed?
"Drink." And they drink to Jesus and are borne to bed.
He teacheth them to sell. "We need coin for our draught.
"How shall we bring the price, since ye give naught for naught?
"We crave the fire drink now."—"Friends, let not that prevent.
"We lend on all your harvests, take our cent. per cent."
"Sirs, but the crop is gone."—"There is your land in lots."
"The land? It was our fathers'."—"Curse ye for idle sots,
"A rascal lazing pack. Have ye no hands to work?
"Off to the mines and dig, and see it how ye shirk."—
"As slaves?" "No, not as *slaves*. Our principles forbid.
"*Free labourers*, if you will. We use that word instead.
"The 'dignity of labour' ye shall learn for hire.
"No paltering. No excuse. The white man hates a liar,
"And hates a grumbling hand. Enough if we provide
"Tools with the drink and leave your backs with a whole hide.
"These lands are ours by Charter. If you doubt it, bring
"Your case before the Courts, which will expound the thing.
"As for your women folk. Look, there are ways well known

"All women have of living in a Christian town.
" Moreover you do ill.   One wife the law allows,
" And you, you say, have four.   Send three round to our house."
—Thus is Thy gospel preached.   Its issue, Lord, behold
In the five Continents, the new world and the old.
The happier tribes of Man despoiled, enslaved, betrayed
To the sole white Man's lust, husband and wife and maid.
Their laughter drowned in tears, their kindness in mad wrath,
Their dignity of joy in a foul trance of death,
Till at the last they turn and in their anguish rend.
Then loud the cry goeth forth, the white man's to each friend:
"Help! Christians, to our help!   These black fiends murder us."
And the last scene is played in death's red charnel house.
The Saxon anger flames.   His ships in armament
Bear slaughter on their wings.   The Earth with fire is rent,
And the poor souls misused are wiped from the world's face
In one huge imprecation from the Saxon race,
In one huge burst of prayer and insolent praise to Thee,
Lord God, for Thy high help and proved complicity.
Nay Lord, 'tis not a lie, the thing I tell Thee thus.
Their bishops in their Churches lead, incredulous,
The public thanks profane.   They sanctify the sword—
" Te Deum laudamus.   Give peace in our time, O Lord."
Hast Thou not heard their chanting?   Nay, Thou dost not
        hear,
Or Thou hadst loosed Thy hand like lightning in the clear
To smite their ribald lips with palsy, these false priests,

These Lords who boast Thine aid at their high civic feasts,
The ignoble shouting crowds, the prophets of their Press,
Pouring their daily flood of bald self-righteousness,
Their poets who write big of the "White Burden." Trash !
The White Man's Burden, Lord, is the burden of his cash.
—There. Thou hast heard the truth. Thy world, Lord God
    of Heaven,
Lieth in the hands of thieves who pillage morn and even.
And Thou still sleepest on ! Nay but Thou needs must hear
Or abdicate Thy name of High Justiciar
Henceforward and for ever. It o'erwhelmeth Thee
With more than temporal shame. Thy silence is a Sea
Crying through all the spheres in pain and ceasing not
As blood from out the ground to mark crime's murder spot :
" There is no hope—no truth. He hath betrayed the trust.
" The Lord God is unjust. The Lord God is unjust."

                                              (A cry without.)
This is their cry in Heaven who give Thee service true.
Arise, Lord, and avenge as was Thy wont to do.

        (The Angels re-enter in disorder, weeping).

The Lord God

What tears be these, my Sons ? What ails ye that ye weep ?
Speak, Shepherds of the flock ! Ye that have cared my sheep,
Ye that are charged with Man. Is it as this One saith ?
Is Satan then no liar who loudly witnesseth
Man's ruin of the World ?

THE ANGEL OF PITY (*coming forward*)
                                Lord, it is even so
Thy Earth is a lost force, Man's lazar-house of woe,
Undone by his lewd will.   We may no longer strive.
The evil hath prevailed.   There is no soul alive
That shall escape his greed.   We spend our days in tears
Mourning Thy world's lost beauty in the night of years.
All pity is departed.   Each once happy thing
That on Thy fair Earth went, how fleet of foot or wing,
How glorious in its strength, how wondrous in design,
How royal in its raiment tinctured opaline,
How rich in joyous life, the inheritor of forms
All noble, all of worth, which had survived the storms,
The chances of decay in the World's living plan,
From the remote fair past when still ignoble Man
On his four foot-soles went and howled through the lone hills
In moody bestial wrath, unclassed among Earth's ills—
Each one of them is doomed.   From the deep Central Seas
To the white Poles, Man ruleth pitiless Lord of these,
And daily he destroyeth.   The great whales he driveth
Beneath the northern ice, and quarter none he giveth,
Who perish there of wounds in their huge agony.
He presseth the white bear on the white frozen sea
And slaughtereth for his pastime.   The wise amorous seal
He flayeth big with young, the walrus cubs that kneel
But cannot turn his rage, alive he mangleth them,
Leaveth in breathing heaps, outrooted branch and stem.

44

In every land he slayeth. He hath new engines made
Which no life may withstand, nor in the forest shade
Nor in the sunlit plain, which wound all from afar,
The timorous with the valiant, waging his false war,
Coward, himself unseen. In pity, Lord, look down
On the blank widowed plains which he hath made his own
By right of solitude. Where, Lord God, are they now,
Thy glorious bison herds, Thy ariels white as snow,
Thy antelopes in troops, the zebras of Thy plain?
Behold their whitened bones on the dull track of men.
Thy elephants, Lord, where? For ages thou didst build
Their frames' capacity, the hide which was their shield
No thorn might pierce, no sting, no violent tooth assail,
The tusks which were their levers, the lithe trunk their flail.
Thou strengthenedst their deep brain. Thou madest them wise
    to know
And wiser to ignore, advised, deliberate, slow,
Conscious of power supreme in right. The manifest token
Of Thy high will on earth, Thy natural peace unbroken,
Unbreakable by fear. For ages did they move
Thus, kings of Thy deep forest swayed by only love.
Where are they now, Lord God? A fugitive spent few
Used as Man's living targets by the ignoble crew
Who boast their coward skill to plant the balls that fly.
Thy work of all time spoiled, their only use to die
That these sad clowns may laugh. Nay, Lord, we weep for *Thee*,
And spend ourselves in tears for Thy marred majesty.

Behold, Lord, what we bring—this last proof in our hands,
Their latest fiendliest spoil from Thy fair tropic lands,
The birds of all the Earth unwinged to deck the heads
Of their unseemly women ; plumage of such reds
As not the sunset hath, such purples as no throne,
Not even in heaven, showeth,—hardly, Lord, Thine own ;
Such azures as the sea's, such greens as are in Spring
The oak trees' tenderest buds of watched-for blossoming,
Such opalescent pearls as only in Thy skies
The lunar bow revealeth to night's sleep-tired eyes.
Behold them, Lord of Beauty, Lord of Reverence,
Lord of Compassion, Thou who meetest means to ends,
Nor madest Thy world fair for less than Thine own fame,
Behold Thy birds of joy lost, tortured, put to shame
For these vile strumpets' whim.   Arise, or cease to be
Judge of the quick and dead !   These dead wings cry to Thee !
Arise, Lord, and avenge !

THE ANGELS
We wait upon Thy word.
(*The Lord God covereth His face.*)

SATAN
Thou hearest them, Lord God.

THE LORD GOD
Good Satan, I have heard.
Thou art more just than I—alas, more just than I.

46

THE ANGELS
Behold the Lord God weepeth.

THE ANGEL OF PITY
What eyes should be dry
If for a crime eyes weep? This crime transcendeth crime.
And the Lord God hath pity—in His own good time.

THE LORD GOD
Alas, the time is late. I do repent Me sore
The wrong I did thee, Satan, in those griefs of yore.
The wrong I did the Earth. Yet is Eternity
A long day for atonement. Thou thyself shalt be
My instrument here of wrath to purge this race of Man
And cast him on Time's dunghill, whence he first began.
What, Angel, is thy counsel? Shall we unseal again
The fountains of the heavens, send our outpoured rain,
And flood him with new waters? Shall it be by fire?
Shall we embraize the earth in one vast funeral pyre
By impact of a star? let loose a sulphurous wind?
Belch rocks from the Earth's bowels? Shall we strike Man blind
With an unbearable light? Shall we so shake the hills,
The plains, that he fall palsied, grind him in the mills
Of a perpetual hail, importune him with snow,
Scourge him with noise unceasing, or the glutinous flow
Of a long pestilent stench? Speak, Satan, all thy thought,
Thou who the traitor knowest. How may he be brought
Best to annihilation?

SATAN

Lord, by none of these,
Thy floods, Thy flames, Thy storms were puerilities.
He hath too large a cunning to be taken thus.
He would outride Thy waves, outblast Thy sulphurous
Winds with his counter-winds. He liveth on foul air
As on the breath of heaven. He hath nor thought nor care
For Thy worst lightning strokes, holding their principle
Rock-firm in his own hand. All natural powers fulfil
His brain's omnipotence. He standeth at each point
Armed for defiant war in harness without joint.
Though Thou shouldst break the Earth in twain he should not
    bend.
Thou needest a force to aid Thee, an ally, a friend,
A principle of good which shall outwit his guile
With true white guilelessness, his anger with a smile,
His force with utter weakness. Only thus, Lord God,
Shalt Thou regain Thy Earth, a purified abode,
And rid it of the Human.

THE LORD GOD

                        And the means? Thy plan
Needeth a new redemption.

SATAN

                        Ay, but not of Man.
He is beyond redeeming, or Thy Son had died

Not wholly to this loss. Who would be crucified
To-day must choose another, a young fleshly form,
Free from the simian taint, were it but flower or worm,
Or limpet of the rock, or grieving nightingale,
Wherein to preach his gospel. Yet should he prevail,
If only for truth's sake and that this latest lie
Should be laid bare to shame, Time's fraud, Humanity.
Choose Thee an Angel, Lord; it were enough. Thy Son
Was a price all too great even had the world been won.
Nor can it be again. An Angel shall suffice
For Thy new second sending, so Thou guide the choice
To a more reasoned issue—so Thou leave Mankind
Henceforth to his sole ways as at his outset, blind
To all but his own lusts, untutored by Thy grace.
This is the road, Lord God. I bow before Thy face.
I make Thee my submission to do all Thy will,
So Thou absolve and pardon.

The Lord God

O incomparable
Good servant, Satan, thou art absolved indeed.
It was *thy* right to pardon thy God's lack of heed,
His wrath at thy wise counsel. Nay, thou shamest Me.
Be thou absolved, good Angel, Ego absolvo te
Ab omnibus peccatis. Once more be it thy right
To stand before God's throne for ever in His sight,
And trusted more than these. Speak, Satan, what thou wilt,

All shall be granted thee, the glory with the guilt
Of the Earth lost and won.   Who is it thou wouldst send
Agent and messenger to work to this new end?
What Angel of them all?   I pledge thee My full faith
It shall be as thou wilt.

SATAN

Who goeth must die the death,
Since death is all life's law, and taste of corporal pain.
And whoso dieth must die, nor think to live again.

THE LORD GOD

Shall it be Michael?   Speak.

SATAN

Nay, Lord, nor Gabriel.
They are Thy servants tried, who love Thy Heaven too well.
Thou shalt not drive them forth to the wild wastes of Earth.
What should they do, Lord God, with a terrestrial birth,
With less than Thy long joys?   Nay, rather choose Thee one
Already marred with grief with Time's disunion,
One all too sad for Heaven, to whom Eternity
Is as a charge o'erspent, who hath no fear to die,
But gladly would lie down and be for aye no more,
The flotsam of Time's waves upon Death's outer shore,
Forgotten and forgetting.   Grant me, Lord God, this,
In penance for the past, Death's full forgetfulness.

THE LORD GOD

And thou wouldst be incarnate ?

SATAN

                    As the least strong thing,
The frailest, the most fond, an insect on the wind,
Which shall prevail by love, by ignorance, by lack
Of all that Man most trusteth to secure his back,
To arm his hand with might. What Thy Son dreamed of Man
Will I work out anew as some poor cateran,
The weakest of the Earth, with only beauty's power
And Thy good grace to aid, the creature of an hour
Too fugitive for fight, too frail even far to fly,
And at the hour's end, Lord, to close my wings and die.
Such were the new redemption.

THE LORD GOD

                    Thou good angel ! Nay
The World were all unworthy such high price to pay.
I will not have thee die.

SATAN

                    'Tis not for the World's sake,
Lord God of Heaven and Earth, that I petition make,
But for Thy justice foiled. It irketh me to know
That I have tutored Man against Thee, to this woe,
And given him sure success. Yet is the World's self good,
And I would prove it Thee, lest Man's ingratitude

Should so affect all truth; all honour, all high faith,
That Thou Thyself, Lord God, shouldst fall a prey to death
And leave him in dominion.   What to me were Heaven
With this thought unappeased—even thus absolved, forgiven,
Yet by myself condemned ?

                    THE LORD GOD
                              Ah, Satan.   Thy old pride
Still lingereth in the clefts.   Yet art thou not denied
Since I have sworn thee faith.   Go, thou good messenger
And God's peace go with thee.   Ho! ye without!   Give ear.
Bow down to the Lord Satan, Our anointed priest,
The new incarnate Word.

                    THE ANGELS
                    All hail!

                    MICHAEL (aside)
                              The Antichrist!

PRINTED BY R. FOLKARD AND SON, 22, DEVONSHIRE STREET, QUEEN SQUARE, LONDON, W.C.

www.ingramcontent.com/pod-product-compliance
Lightning Source LLC
Chambersburg PA
CBHW031747090426
42739CB00008B/921